Unsolved Mysteries

The Cosmic Joker

Brian Innes

RSVP

RAINTREE
STECK-VAUGHN
PUBLISHERS
A Steck-Vaughn Company

Austin, Texas

www.steck-vaughn.com

Developed by Brown Partworks
Editor: Lindsey Lowe
Designer: Joan Curtis
Picture Researcher: Brigitte Arora

Raintree Steck-Vaughn Publishers Staff
Project Manager: Joyce Spicer
Editor: Pam Wells

Library of Congress Cataloging-in-Publication Data
Innes, Brian.
    The cosmic joker/by Brian Innes.
        p.   cm.—(Unsolved mysteries)
    Includes bibliographical references and index.
    Summary: Details the work of American writer Charles Fort and others who
recorded events that had no scientific explanation, such as objects falling from
the sky, human psychic powers, unusual disappearances, and odd coincidences.
    ISBN 0-8172-5487-0 (Hardcover)
    ISBN 0-8172-5849-3 (Softcover)
    1. Science—Miscellanea—Juvenile literature. 2. Fort, Charles, 1874-1932—
Juvenile literature. [1. Science—Miscellanea. 2. Curiosities and wonders.
3. Fort, Charles, 1874-1932.] I. Title. II. Series: Innes, Brian. Unsolved
mysteries.
Q173.I55   1999
001.94—dc21   98-35242
                                               CIP   AC
Printed and bound in the United States
1 2 3 4 5 6 7 8 9 0 WZ 02 01 00 99 98

Acknowledgments

Cover: David Robbins/Tony Stone Images; **Page 5:** Fortean Picture Library; **Page 6:** Charles Fort Institute/Fortean Picture Library; **Page 7:** Hulton-Deutsch Collection/Corbis; **Page 8:** Patrick Ward/Corbis; **Page 9:** Hulton Getty Images; **Page 11:** Darrell Gulin/Corbis; **Page 13:** Dave Bartruff/Corbis; **Page 14:** Fortean Picture Library; **Page 15:** Reading Evening Post; **Page 16:** George Post/Science Photo Library; **Page 17:** Stephen Frink/Corbis; **Page 18:** Dave G. Houser/Corbis; **Page 19:** Ralph White/Corbis; **Page 21:** Kevin R. Morris/Corbis; **Page 22:** Kobal Collection; **Page 23:** UPI/Corbis-Bettmann; **Page 25:** Mary Evans Picture Library; **Page 26:** Hulton Getty Images; **Page 28:** Library of Congress/Corbis; **Pages 29 and 30:** Mary Evans Picture Library; **Page 31:** Charles E. Rotkin/Corbis; **Page 33:** Gary Parker/Science Photo Library; **Page 34:** William A. Bake/Corbis; **Page 36:** Mirror Syndication International; **Page 37:** Dr. Susan Blackmore/Fortean Picture Library; **Page 38:** Leicester Mercury; **Page 40:** Neil Rabinowitz/Corbis; **Page 41:** Library of Congress/Corbis; **Page 43:** Seattle Art Museum/Corbis; **Page 44:** Harry Rountree/Mary Evans Picture Library; **Page 45:** Robbie Jack/Corbis; **Page 46:** Roger Wilmshurst; FLPA/Corbis.

Contents

The World of Charles Fort

Charles Fort was fascinated by the universe. He spent his life trying to explain why strange things happen.

The cover from an issue of the **Fortean Times** *(opposite).* The magazine, which began in 1973, prints reports of any unusual happenings.

The world is full of unusual events that cannot be explained, and some are stranger than others. People claim to have seen animals, eggs, stones, and other things falling from a clear sky. And nearly everybody can tell you about an amazing coincidence that they have experienced.

Today the word *Fortean* is used to describe the collection and study of any unexplained happenings. It takes its name from Charles Hoy Fort, who spent his life trying to find out the reasons for such events.

WISE WORDS

Fort was born in 1874 in Albany, New York. Both his parents were originally from Holland. They came to the United States to start a new life. At the age of 18, Fort decided to leave home. He set out to travel around the world.

When he finally returned home, he told a neighbor about his travels. Because this man was very old, he had spent many years unable to move from his bed. He told Fort that he, too, had once traveled. However, he also said that he had only just begun to get the most out of his experiences. This had happened since his life

Fortean Times

ISSUE No.46 | The Foremost Journal of Strange Phenomena | PRICE: £1.50 $3.00

SPECIAL ISSUE: LAKE MONSTERS

The Fortean Times ... to this day, collects reports of strange happenings from all over the world.

Charles Fort. He tried to find reasons for the mysteries of the world right up until his death in 1932.

had become limited to his bedroom. Later Fort remembered these words. He realized it was better to focus on one thing in life, rather than try to do a bit of everything.

In an effort to follow this advice, Fort settled in the Bronx, a borough of New York City. For 20 years he wrote for a newspaper. He spent all his spare time reading. He read scientific books and magazines, as well as the world's major news-papers. He became very interested in any reports of events that seemed to have no scientific explanation. He wrote them down.

TAKING NOTES

Fort made about 25,000 notes on small squares of paper. Then he burned them all saying, "They were not what I wanted." He began again. When he had made many thousands of notes, he wrote two books. One book was called *X*. The story was about people on Mars who controlled events on Earth. The other book was called *Y*. It was about a strange civilization living at the South Pole in the Antarctic. Around this time, Fort met and became friends with American writer Theodore Dreiser.

In 1917 Charles Fort's uncle died. Fort was left just enough money to be able to give up his job. He no longer had to work for a living. In 1970 author Damon Knight published a book about Fort's life. He wrote: "He was an utterly peaceable . . . man. He lived quietly with his wife, almost never went out or had visitors. He spent the mornings working at home and the afternoons in the library."

USEFUL CONTACT

Fort could not find anybody to print X and Y. He burned his manuscripts. Almost at once, however, he began work on a new book. When Theodore Dreiser read the manuscript, he liked it. Dreiser arranged for it to be published. This was a book all about unusual happenings. It went on sale in 1919.

In his book, Fort gives the facts of the stories, then follows these up with his own opinion of them. He also gives the opinions of or explanations by many scientific experts. Fort was amazed at how scientists refused to believe in anything that they could not explain. He found they did not believe his stories.

As if poking fun at the scientists for their lack of wonder at the world, Fort said: "One measures a circle beginning anywhere." He meant that it didn't matter where you started. One fact would always be related to another.

Theodore Dreiser believed in the world of Charles Fort. This picture of Dreiser was taken in 1931, the year the Fortean Society was founded.

Most people who read Fort's first published book did not know what to make of it or simply did not believe it. Fort was angry and again burned his notes—all 40,000 of them! Then he took a ship to England.

LONDON LIFE

Fort visited the British Museum in London. There he found a huge collection of books and magazines on unexplained happenings. He began to make notes again. For the next eight years, he and his wife lived just a few hundred yards from the museum. He began to believe in space travel. Sometimes he spoke on the subject at London's "Speaker's Corner," on the edge of Hyde Park. Anybody who has something to say can stand there and speak to anyone willing to listen.

During his time in London, Fort wrote *New Lands*, an attack on the beliefs of astronomers. Astronomers

This is the Reading Room of the British Museum. When Fort arrived in London he spent many hours in this room. The museum had a huge collection of writings on unexplained events.

While he was in England, Fort gave speeches at Speaker's Corner in Hyde Park. This man (above) was a well-known face at the "Corner" throughout the 1930s.

are scientists who study the movement and positions of the planets and stars. They, also, refused to believe his ideas about space travel.

In 1929 Fort and his wife returned to New York. There he wrote a third book, titled *Lo!* This was mainly about unusual objects falling from the sky—coins, frogs, worms, shells, and snails! His last book, *Wild Talents*, was completed in 1932. This covered reports of human psychic powers, unexplained disappearances, and other mysteries.

BACK HOME

During this time Fort had been losing his sight. He was also becoming weak. Right up to the end of his life, Fort continued to make notes. His last note read: "Difficulty shaving. Gaunt [thin and bony] places in face." On May 3, 1932, Charles Fort was taken to the hospital, where he died. Sixty thousand of his notes were later given to the New York Public Library.

THE FORTEAN SOCIETY

In 1931 Dreiser and Tiffany Thayer, another writer, had started the Fortean Society. They wanted other people to study Fort's ideas about mysterious events. Fort himself, however, refused to be the society's president. Some years before, he had written: "The great trouble is that the majority of persons who are attracted are the ones we do not want." Fort was not interested in people who were just trying to prove scientists wrong. He wanted to attract people who were interested in finding out about the universe.

The cosmic force did not seem to be particularly interested in what was fair!

The Fortean Society was successful for more than 25 years. It ended when Tiffany Thayer died in 1959. However, all Charles Fort's books went on sale again in 1974. And, in 1973, the *Fortean Times* was started in London. It is a magazine that, to this day, collects reports of strange happenings from all over the world.

A HUGE COSMIC JOKE

As early as 1917, Fort had begun making notes on lights and on dark objects that had been seen moving and hovering in the skies over many countries. We now call such objects Unidentified Flying Objects, or UFOs. Fort thought that some of these objects might be alien spacecraft. Again, scientists laughed at him.

Fort also came up with the word teleportation— which means "moving things over distances, without any known force." He believed teleportation was one of the basic forces of nature. This "cosmic force," he claimed, had distributed life-forms among the planets. Perhaps it could explain some of the mysteries of the world. Once again, the scientific world laughed at him. Fort, however, refused to be put off by this.

THE GREAT AND THE SMALL

Fort suggested that at the time when the world was being formed, this unknown cosmic force must have been very strong. It caused islands to vanish beneath the sea and continents to split from one another. Fort pointed out the bizarre nature of this amazing event. He noted that this force had created the great Rocky Mountains. Then, as it died down, it had simply tossed a few pebbles at farmers in New Jersey! Fort found the picture amusing—the grand landscape of the Rockies standing in contrast to a patch of stony farmland.

It appeared that the cosmic force did not seem to be particularly interested in what was fair! And so the idea of the "Cosmic Joker" was born.

Fort thought a cosmic joker had a hand in creating the Rocky Mountains (above).

Cosmic Jokes

Bob Rickard was an editor of the *Fortean Times* magazine. In 1977 he and a man named John Michell wrote a book together. This book was titled *A Book of Wonders*. It continued the work of Charles Fort by bringing together various stories about unexplained happenings.

Rickard had always liked Fort's words, "the cosmic humor of it all." In his book, Rickard also noted the extremely bizarre nature of many unexplained events. They had to be more than just coincidences. According to Rickard, many people think there is some mysterious force that causes things to happen on Earth. It has a sense of humor and likes to poke fun at us. Because of this, the force has been called the "cosmic joker."

FAVORITE TALES

One of Rickard's favorite stories is about Carol Alspaugh, from Grand Rapids, Michigan. Early one morning in the winter of 1979, Alspaugh noticed a large icicle hanging outside her kitchen window. It was shaped something like a human hand. Part of it was broken.

Alspaugh's sister was going to have surgery on her hand that same day. However, the doctors

An icicle something like this (opposite) was to take on a special meaning for Carol Alspaugh in the winter of 1979.

. . . Alspaugh noticed a large icicle hanging outside her kitchen window.

had to cancel her operation at the last minute because she had injured her arm. The new injury had been caused by an icicle that had fallen on her!

FLYING OMELETTES!

Another story in Rickard's book was even more unusual. In December 1974, eggs began to fall from a clear blue sky in Wokingham, Berkshire, England. They crashed down on cars, fences, and the roof and playground of a school. Local people jokingly said they were UFOs—in this case meaning Unidentified Flying Omelettes! Some of the schoolchildren even picked up whole, unbroken eggs. The name of the school was Keep Hatch.

Such strange events have led many people to think that there must be some mysterious, unknown force behind happenings of this kind. But how can a force have a sense of humor?

Bob Rickard in 1991. In 1977 he wrote a book with John Michell. The book describes all kinds of cosmic jokes that would have amused Charles Fort.

These children from Keep Hatch school are holding up some of the eggs that mysteriously rained down on their playground in December 1974.

APRIL SHOWERS

On the morning of April 22, 1949, Dr. A.D. Bajkov, of Marksville, Louisiana, was hit by hundreds of fish that suddenly fell out of the sky. Dr. Bajkov was an expert on animals and fish. He said the fish that fell on his head were sunfish, minnows, and black bass. But the nearest ocean was over 80 miles (129 km) away.

On April 2, 1973, a weather expert was walking near Manchester, England. He was nearly knocked over by a large block of ice that fell from the sky and smashed at his feet. Because he was a weather expert, he was able to carry out tests on the ice. But can it have been pure chance that the ice fell at the feet of someone who knew how to do this? What a pity it had not happened on April 1!

These were not the first stories about unusual things suddenly falling out of the sky. Charles Fort

This is a hailstorm cloud in the desert. This type of cloud is known as a cumulonimbus cloud. Particles of rain and snow are pulled up into the cloud. Strong winds within the cloud cause these and other particles to stick together as hailstones. The cloud floats until it becomes too heavy to be supported by the air currents. Hailstones then fall to Earth. Could this be an explanation for some of the strange things that have suddenly fallen from clear blue skies?

had discovered many reports about stories something like these. Lumps of meat had rained down from a clear blue sky in Bath County, Kentucky, on March 3, 1876. They were scattered over 5,000 square yards (4,180 sq m). They turned out to be pieces of horse meat. Local people suggested that the meat had been dropped by buzzards, which are large birds of prey, or hunting birds that feed on animals. However, it would have taken hundreds of birds to drop so much food, and none had been seen in the area.

At Dubuque, Iowa, there was a bad hailstorm on June 16, 1882. Some of the hailstones were as big as 5 inches (12.8 cm) across. Two of the hailstones had small living frogs inside them. On May 11, 1894, a block of ice fell on Bovina, 8 miles (12.8 km) east of Vicksburg, Mississippi. It had a turtle inside it!

A storm struck the town of Worcester, England, on May 28, 1881. Hundreds of shellfish came crashing down with the rain. Some fell with such force that they buried themselves in the ground. People rushed out to collect them. One large shell was found to contain a living crab. But Worcester is some 70 miles (112.6 km) from the sea.

HEAVY RAIN

In the spring of 1956, a small dark cloud was seen forming in the sky near Uniontown, Alabama. Soon afterward, there was a shower lasting 15 minutes. Rain fell over a small area—no more than 200 square feet (18.6 sq m). As it fell, the cloud turned white. Hundreds of fish were left wriggling on the ground.

On July 12, 1961, a crop of unripe peaches hurled itself at some workmen at Shreveport, Louisiana. The men were certain that they had not been thrown by anybody. Nobody else was anywhere near them. They said the peaches had come from the sky.

A shoal of minnows. Many of the cosmic jokes that Rickard described involved fish falling from the sky!

Most remarkable of all was the animal that fell from the sky at Evansville, Indiana, on May 21, 1911. This was a young alligator some 2 feet (0.6 m) long. It landed on the doorstep of a woman named Mrs. Hiram Winchell. She was very surprised! However, when the animal began to crawl into her house Mrs. Winchell's surprise turned to fear, and she killed it.

17

This is Bermuda, where the easiest way to get around is by small motorcycle. However, with the Cosmic Joker around it may not necessarily be the safest.

THE JOKES TURN BAD

These events are almost like the jokes that children like to play on one another. Bob Rickard thinks the Cosmic Joker has a very childlike sense of humor. It often seems to want to surprise or shock people.

Sometimes, for example, people have had the same experience more than once. In Detroit, Michigan, a baby fell 14 stories from an apartment balcony. It fell on Joseph Figlock. A year later exactly the same thing happened to him again! Fortunately in both cases the babies and Figlock were unharmed.

Other happenings do not end so well. In Bermuda a man riding a small motorcycle was killed by a taxi, which knocked him off his motorcycle. A year later the man's brother was riding the same motorcycle in the same street. He was also killed—amazingly by the same driver who had killed his brother. It was also the same taxi, and it was carrying the same passenger.

18

ALL IN THE NAME

There seems to be something about the names of people that affects their lives. Dr. Don Triplett was a child expert and helped with the birth of three sets of triplets. Two doctors working together were named Payne and Kilmore. Dr. W. Roy Phang was a dental surgeon. One day a group of British sailors in Hong Kong decided to look up names in the local telephone directory. They found an insurance company called Fu Ling U, a pianomaker named Lo Kee, and a restaurant called Man Sik. Rod Parkes, who lived in Hong Kong, later added several more to the list. They included the Hop On bicycle factory.

A DIFFERENT MYSTERY SOLVED?

Sometimes people are unaware of the humor to be found in names. One of the most famous monsters in the world is said to live in Loch Ness, in Scotland. The monster has never been found. However, during the 1960s and 1970s, a number of people tried to take photographs of the monster using underwater cameras. Sir Peter Scott, the British animal expert, decided to give the Loch Ness monster a proper scientific name. He called it *Nessiteras rhombopteryx*, which means "creature of Ness, with diamond-shaped flippers." Incredibly, someone pointed out that the letters could be changed around so that they read "monster hoax [trick] by Sir Peter S!"

A diver searches for the famous Loch Ness monster in 1976. It has never been found.

19

Just by Chance?

Sometimes things happen that seem beyond belief. But can there be more to such events than first meets the eye?

Everybody experiences a coincidence at some time or other. A coincidence takes place when two or more events that happen by accident seem to have some connection. It could be, for example, that somebody's parents were born in the same town on the same day. This is simply a coincidence, and there is generally nothing more unusual to it than that.

However, sometimes a coincidence is so odd that it seems as if it must have been planned. As Bob Rickard, editor of the *Fortean Times*, once wrote: "Many people feel that there must be some 'cosmic' intelligence [thinking being], with a mischievous sense of humor, behind it."

MORE THAN A JOKE

One day George D. Bryson was making a trip from the South to New York City by railroad. It was only as his train pulled into Louisville, Kentucky, that he decided to get off the train and visit the town.

Bryson had never been to Louisville before and knew nobody there. He asked for the name of the best hotel and made his way to it. He was given Room 307. As a joke he said to the desk

A railroad over the Ohio River in Louisville, Kentucky (opposite). When George Bryson stopped off in Louisville, he had the surprise of his life!

20

. . . sometimes a coincidence is so odd that it seems as if it must have been planned.

Goldie Hawn and Anthony Hopkins in the 1974 film The Girl from Petrovka. *Hopkins had experienced a strange coincidence in connection with this film.*

clerk, "Any mail for me?" He was amazed when the clerk handed over a letter that was addressed to "George D. Bryson, Room 307." Another George D. Bryson had stayed in the room before him.

FULL CIRCLE

The Welsh actor Anthony Hopkins has starred in many famous plays and movies. In 1971 he agreed to appear in a film based on George Feifer's book *The Girl from Petrovka*. Hopkins searched all the bookshops of London for a copy of the book. He could not find one. Then, as he set off for home, he spotted a copy of the book lying on a seat in the subway station at Leicester Square. It had been left there by another traveler. Hopkins took it home.

Two years later Anthony Hopkins was working on the movie in Vienna, Austria. One day George Feifer visited the set. He mentioned that he did not have any copies of his own book. He had lent his last one to a friend who had lost it. "Is this it?" asked Hopkins. There were notes written on the pages. It was Feifer's own lost copy!

STORY WITH A TWIST

Another book caught the attention of the FBI. This was a book about a kidnapping. It was written by Harrison James. His real name was James Rusk, Jr. The book, which was published in 1972, told the story of a group of terrorists. They had kidnapped a student named Patricia, who was the daughter of a famous wealthy person. The girl was taken from her college campus. Her boyfriend was beaten up by the terrorists, but was thought to have had something to do with her kidnapping. At the end of the book, Patricia became a member of the terrorist gang. By then she had come to believe in the ideas they were fighting for.

On February 4, 1974, a woman named Patricia Hearst was kidnapped. She was taken from the Berkeley campus at the University of California. Patricia, known as Patty, was the granddaughter of the wealthy newspaper owner William Randolph Hearst. It turned out that Patty had been kidnapped

Patty Hearst and two U.S. marshals on their way to court in 1976. She was eventually found guilty of helping the terrorist group that had kidnapped her.

by some members of a terrorist group led by Donald DeFreeze. Her boyfriend, Steven Weed, was beaten up. Nevertheless, the FBI thought that he must have had something to do with the kidnapping. The FBI thought that the coincidence between this event and Rusk's book was just too great. For a while they even thought that Rusk was involved in the kidnapping.

. . . the ship hit an iceberg off the American coast. It sank with terrible loss of life.

Donald DeFreeze sent tapes to the newspapers. On these tapes Patty Hearst spoke out in support of the terrorists. On April 15 she was photographed taking part in an armed robbery of a bank in California. On May 17, DeFreeze and five of his group were killed by police during a gun battle in a Los Angeles suburb. Patty Hearst escaped with some other members of the group. On September 18, 1975, she was finally captured. The following year she was found guilty of helping the terrorists and was put in prison. She was released in February 1979.

STRANGER THAN FICTION

The Patty Hearst story was not the first coincidence to involve the story of a book. Much earlier the story told in another book and the events that followed later were even more amazing.

In 1898 the American writer Morgan Robertson wrote a story titled *Futility*. He described the building of a great ocean liner named *Titan*. One April night the ship hit an iceberg off the American coast. It sank with terrible loss of life. In his book, Robertson described many details about the ship and gave the number of passengers who died.

Fourteen years later the British liner *Titanic* was on its first voyage across the Atlantic from England to New York. On a freezing April night, the *Titanic* ran into an iceberg. The ship, along with most of the passengers and crew, were lost. The facts were almost exactly the same as in Robertson's story.

But that was not the end of it. One April night in 1935, a ship named *Titanian* was sailing from England to Canada. One of the ship's crew members, William Reeves, realized that the ship was in the same part of

This is a painting of the great ship Titanic *as it ran into an iceberg on the freezing night of April 14, 1912. The* Titanian *had better luck in 1935.*

the ocean where both the fictional *Titan* and the real *Titanic* had sunk. Further, Reeves had been born on April 15, 1912—hours before the *Titanic* sank!

Without thinking, Reeves shouted that there was danger ahead. A few seconds later *Titanian* brushed against a giant iceberg as it suddenly appeared out of the darkness. Luckily the ship did not hit the iceberg hard enough to cause major damage.

HISTORY REPEATING ITSELF

Toward the end of the 19th century, a coincidence happened to the family of a well-known actor. It was something like what happened to Anthony Hopkins many years later.

The actor was Edward A. Sothern. He was a friend of the Prince of Wales—the future king of England, Edward VII. The two men regularly went hunting

Edward VII and a shooting party in Norfolk, England, in 1909. While he was still the Prince of Wales, he had given a friend a matchbox made of gold.

together. One day the prince gave Sothern a gift. It was a small gold matchbox. For some time Sothern kept the matchbox on the chain that attached his pocket watch to his vest. Then one day he lost the matchbox after he was thrown from his horse.

He showed Lawrence the letter and told him the story of the matchbox. On hearing this, . . .

Sothern was sad that he had lost his expensive gift. He had a copy made of it. Later he gave this to his son Lytton, who was also an actor. Lytton went on a tour of Australia, and while he was there he gave the matchbox to a friend named Labertouche.

Twenty years after the original gold matchbox was lost, Lytton Sothern was touring the United States. During the tour he received a letter from his brother George. In this letter George told Lytton that their father's original matchbox had been found by a farm worker. In fact, it was found not very far from where their father had lost it.

PERFECT TIMING

Lytton read the letter on a train. He was with another actor, Arthur Lawrence. Lytton had met him for the first time that same day. He showed Lawrence the letter and told him the story of the matchbox. On hearing this, Lawrence pulled out his watchchain. There was the copy of the matchbox. He said that a man named Labertouche had given it to him several years before. Lytton couldn't believe his eyes.

The great hurricane that hit Galveston, Texas, in 1900 destroyed buildings and killed many people. It also washed the coffin of Charles Francis Coghlan out to sea. Eight years later it arrived just off the shore of his place of birth.

ROOM WITH A VIEW

Arthur Butterworth, a British soldier, had an equally amazing experience during World War II. One day he ordered a music book from a London store that sold secondhand, or used, books. He asked if the book could be mailed to him at the army camp in Taverham Hall, Norfolk, England.

Butterworth was standing by the window of his hut when the package arrived. He opened it and began to look at his book. Inside the book was a postcard, which had been used for a bookmarker. It had been written on August 4, 1913 (strangely, just one year before Britain entered World War I). When Butterworth turned the postcard over he was surprised to see that the picture was "the exact view I had from my hut window at that very moment!"

28

SPECIAL HOMECOMING

Canadian actor Charles Francis Coghlan was on tour in Texas in 1899. While he was in Galveston, he was suddenly taken ill, and later died. His home was on Prince Edward Island in the Gulf of Saint Lawrence, more than 3,000 miles (4,827 km) away by ship. So he was buried in Galveston, inside a stone-lined vault, or chamber. Under 12 months later, the great hurricane of September 1900 struck Galveston. It completely destroyed the town, and the graveyard was flooded. Coghlan's coffin floated out into the Gulf of Mexico.

Eight years passed. Then, in October 1908, some fishermen from Prince Edward Island spotted a long wooden box floating in the waves near the shore. Charles Coghlan's body had returned to its home. This time the actor was buried in the cemetery of the church where he had been baptized as a baby.

The assassination of King Umberto I on July 29, 1900. His friend Umberto had been killed the day before. Was this a coincidence or the work of the cosmic joker?

DOUBLE TROUBLE

On July 28, 1900, King Umberto I of Italy went to the town of Monza. In the evening he visited a local restaurant for a meal. The owner of the restaurant looked almost exactly like the king. In fact, he could have been his twin. The two men began to talk. They soon

29

Abraham Lincoln was shot by an assassin (above). So was John F. Kennedy. Both were also linked by a series of mysterious coincidences. Unfortunately nobody knew this until after the death of Kennedy in 1963. Could Kennedy's death have been prevented if someone had known?

discovered that they were both named Umberto. Also, they had both been born in the city of Turin on March 14, 1844. They had both married on April 22, 1868. Their wives were each named Margherita, and each had a son named Vittorio! As if all that were not enough, the restaurant had opened on the day of the king's coronation.

The following day the king was sorry to learn that the restaurant owner had died in a shooting accident. He turned to one of his assistants to ask for more details. As he did so, three shots rang out. King Umberto had been killed by an assassin.

THE JOKER IS WILD

Finally, there are the strange coincidences that link the assassinations of Presidents Abraham Lincoln and John F. Kennedy. Both men were shot in the back of the head on a Friday. Both events happened in front of their wives. Both were followed as president by men who were named Johnson: Andrew Johnson, born 1808, and Lyndon Johnson, born 1908.

John Wilkes Booth shot Lincoln in a theater and hid in a barn. Lee Harvey Oswald may have shot Kennedy from a warehouse and did hide in a movie theater.

ALL IN THE NAME

Lincoln's secretary was named John Kennedy. He had advised Lincoln against going to the theater that evening. Kennedy's secretary was named Evelyn Lincoln. She had told Kennedy that he should not go to Dallas. The name Lincoln has seven letters—so does Kennedy. The names Andrew Johnson and Lyndon Johnson each have 13 letters. Both assassins had three names. And the names of both these men were made up of 15 letters!

Lee Harvey Oswald shot at President Kennedy in Dallas. He fired from the Texas School Book Depository—the square building at the top of this picture.

Testing Twins

There are many unusual stories about twins. Could the cosmic joker have a hand in these as well?

A pair of identical twins (opposite). Identical twins are always of the same sex and look very much alike. They may also behave in exactly the same ways.

Some of the most unexpected coincidences occur with twins. There are something like 100 million twins in the world. Around one-third of these are said to be "monozygotic." This means that they have both grown from the same egg. It also means that they are identical, or exactly the same, in appearance. Twins who are not identical have grown from two different eggs.

Most twins are raised together. As children they are often dressed in matching clothes by their parents, and they are usually sent to the same schools. Often, twins seem to have a secret way of understanding each other, without the need for speech.

SEPARATED AT BIRTH

But what about twins who are separated? They may be adopted at birth—or soon after—by different families. When they are still young, their parents may be killed in wars and the children taken to safety by other people. The children might end up in different parts of the world. Often neither knows that he or she has a twin. In those special cases, they are raised in very different surroundings and situations.

Often, twins seem to have a secret way of understanding each other, without the need for speech.

You would expect that in such cases the twins would grow up into adults with totally different ways of life. However, there are many cases where twins who have been separated end up doing the same things in life.

THE TWO JIMS

In Piqua, Ohio, two five-week-old twin boys were adopted by different families in August 1939. One was taken by Jess and Lucille Lewis in Lima. The other was taken by Ernest and Sarah Springer in Dayton, 80 miles (128 km) away. Both sets of new parents were told that the other twin had died.

Six years later Lucille Lewis learned the truth by accident. She had gone to court to fill in some papers about the baby. When the man at the court heard that Mrs. Lewis had named her boy James, he

A quiet neighborhood of St. Petersburg, Florida. Each "Jim twin" had taken many summer vacations in the town without knowing that the other twin was also there.

said: "But you can't do that. They named the other little boy James!" However, "Jim" he remained.

James Springer, also known as Jim, grew up not knowing about his twin. Jim Lewis was told he had a brother. However, it was many years before he decided to find out more. At last the two Jims met.

MEETING THEIR OTHER HALF

Jim Springer and Jim Lewis met each other in 1979, when they were both 39 years old. They found that they had both grown up with brothers named Larry. They had both owned a pet dog named Troy. At school both had hated spelling but enjoyed math.

Their first wives were both named Linda. Their second wives were both named Betty.

Both Jims had been married twice. Their first wives were both named Linda. Their second wives were both named Betty. They called their first-born sons James Alan and James Allan. Both families had taken summer vacations at the same beach in Saint Petersburg, Florida, each driving there in a Chevrolet.

THE SAME PATHS THROUGH LIFE

The two men had both worked as filling station attendants, and for the same fast-food restaurant. Both had been part-time deputy sheriffs. Both had taken up carpentry and drawing as hobbies. When the two families met, they were surprised to find that not only did the two Jims look alike, but they even spoke and behaved in the same way. Perhaps less surprisingly, each man was 6 feet (1.8 m) tall and weighed 180 pounds (81.7 kg). At the age of 18, both Jims had started to suffer from bad headaches that started in the afternoon. Both had problems with their hearts later in life, and both had gained 10 pounds (4.5 kg) in weight at the same time.

Professor Thomas Bouchard, of the University of Minnesota, was interested by reports of the "Jim twins." He decided to study twins that had not grown up together. He discovered many cases during 1979.

BOUCHARD'S BABIES

It was in 1979 that Jeanette Hamilton opened the Sunday paper at her home in Paisley, Scotland. She saw a photograph of herself. However, it was really Irene Reid, who lived 300 miles (482.7 km) away.

Long-lost twins, Jeanette Hamilton and Irene Reid, finally met each other in 1979. Amazingly, at this meeting they were wearing matching clothes.

Many scientific tests have been carried out on twins. They have been found to think and behave the same way. Some also seem to be able to transfer their thoughts to each other. The drawings above and right were done by a pair of identical twins. One twin was asked to draw a picture, and the other twin was asked to try and draw the same picture. Although the drawings are not the same, they both show methods of transportation and travel.

Irene was searching for her long-lost twin. Their mother had given them up for adoption in 1944. When Jeanette and Irene met at last, 35 years later, they found that they not only looked alike, but they had almost the same personality, or ways of behaving and thinking.

Both women were terrified of heights. Both had, at one time, done work for the same beauty product company. They hated water and, if they went to the beach, would sit with their backs to the ocean. Both disliked being in small spaces, and both blinked a lot.

ANOTHER AMAZING MEETING

Also in 1979 Mrs. Bridget Harrison discovered she was the twin of Mrs. Dorothy Lowe. They had been separated in 1944 and lived 200 miles (321.8 km) apart in England. Both had married within a year of each other. One named her son Richard Andrew, and the other Andrew Richard. Their daughters were named

Bridget Harrison and Dorothy Lowe. Like Jeanette Hamilton and Irene Reid, they had been separated in 1944. Professor Thomas Bouchard brought them together again in 1979.

Catherine Louise and Karen—Dorothy had nearly called her daughter Katherine, rather than Karen. Both women had studied piano to the same level. Both liked stuffed toys and had a cat named Tiger. Their wedding dresses had been almost identical, and both wore the same perfume. In 1960 both had kept a diary, but only for that one year. The entries were the same type, day for day.

MORE COINCIDENCES

Another of Bouchard's cases in 1979 was that of Barbara Herbert and Daphne Goodship. They were born in London in 1939. Barbara and her family lived in southern England, while Daphne and her family lived several hundred miles to the north. The new mothers of both girls had died while the girls were still children. Both girls had fallen downstairs at the age of 15. Each had met her future husband at a dance in the town hall when she was age 16. The first child of both Daphne and Barbara died. Each then had two boys, followed by a girl.

When they met for the first time, both were wearing . . . brown velvet jackets.

Daphne and Barbara also found that they often behaved and thought about things in the same way. Both liked carving—Barbara in wood, Daphne in soap. They were both frightened of heights and hated the sight of blood. They liked to read the same kinds of books.

When they met for the first time, both Daphne and Barbara were wearing beige dresses and brown velvet jackets. Both had colored their graying hair the same shade of auburn. They were, of course, physically similar, but their medical history was also the same. There was just one noticeable difference. Daphne had been dieting and was 20 pounds (9 kg) lighter than Barbara.

LONG-DISTANCE TWINS
Professor Bouchard's most amazing case was the story of Oscar Stohr and Jack Yufe. These twins were born in Trinidad, in the West Indies, in 1933. Soon afterward their parents split up. Oscar was

taken to Germany by his mother. He later joined Adolf Hitler's Nazi youth group. Jack was raised in Trinidad by his father, who was a Jewish business-man. When Jack Yufe read about the "Jim twins," he wrote to Bouchard. He asked him to arrange a meeting with his long-lost brother, Oscar. The two brothers met at Minneapolis Airport. They were both wearing glasses with wire rims. They both wore blue shirts, and they had identical mustaches.

UNITED BY BLOOD

Bouchard made a study of the men. He found that they both had all sorts of habits in common. They

A building in Trinidad. Oscar Stohr and Jack Yufe were born on this island.

both kept rubber bands around their wrists. They preferred to eat alone in restaurants because they both liked to read books during meals. They both dipped hot buttered toast into their coffee. When they read magazines, they both read them from the back to the front. One other unusual habit was that they both liked to startle people in elevators by sneezing loudly!

DIVIDED BY WAR

Oscar and Jack walked in the same way. Bouchard was also interested in the fact that, although Oscar

This is a German poster. It is promoting Hitler's Nazi youth group. Oscar Stohr joined the group after being taken to Germany by his mother in the 1930s. His twin remained in Trinidad.

only spoke German and Jack only spoke English, their speech rhythms, or the way in which they spoke, were the same. Bouchard also noted how alike the twins were. This was surprising, given the fact that one had been brought up as a Nazi and the other one as a Jew. During World War II, the Nazis had been responsible for the deaths of millions of Jews in Europe.

TWIN TRAGEDY

Michael and Alex Chisholm were born in Scotland in 1938. Both boys were very healthy as teenagers. At the end of 1955, Michael joined the British Merchant Navy. On December 28, Alex waved goodbye to his twin brother as he set off on his first sea voyage to Egypt. Three days later, 17-year-old Alex celebrated New Year's Eve with his friends. On January 1, 1956, he died suddenly from a heart attack. The news reached Michael on his ship two days later. That night he died unexpectedly in his sleep.

Twins who grow up together will, naturally, have habits in common. But it seems that even when they have been separated there is something that makes their lives follow the same pattern. There are many more stories like these. Are they just mere chance, or are they yet more examples of "cosmic" humor?

A World Trickster

People like to know why things happen. In the past they have created a trickster to blame for things they cannot understand.

This is a raven mask (opposite). The Native American peoples of the Pacific Coast of Canada have many tales about the trickster, Raven.

According to ancient folklore, there is a clever and mischievous being that loves to play tricks on the world. People who study legends and myths call this being the "trickster." In many folktales the trickster is said to look like an animal or a bird. It fools people but in the end it is always found out by its own tricks.

NATIVE AMERICAN FOLKLORE

The Native American peoples have many tales about the trickster. He is known as Bluejay or Mink in the Northwest. On the Pacific Coast of Canada, he is Raven, and the Sioux know him as Spider. In the Great Plains and the Southwest, he is famous as Coyote. And in the Southeast, he is Rabbit, or Hare.

The trickster is said to have existed from the beginning of time. The Blackfoot and Crow called him "Old Man." This meant that he was ageless, as old as Time itself. They did not think that he was really an old man.

Like most of the animals after which it is named, the trickster is foolishly curious. In one story Raven dives to the bottom of the sea to steal fish from a fisherman. He gets caught on

In many folktales the trickster is said to look like an animal or a bird.

Mr. Bear and Brer Rabbit. This picture is from Uncle Remus, *a Brer Rabbit story published in 1908.*

the fishhook. When he struggles to get free, he loses his beak. In another story Coyote pushes his head inside the head of a buffalo and gets stuck.

OTHER TRICKSTERS

In India the same types of stories are told about the Jackal and Hare. In most of Africa, Hare is the hero. It is believed that many of the stories about Hare were taken from Africa to the U.S. by slaves. Joel Chandler Harris's famous books about Brer Rabbit are based on these tales.

In Western Africa the trickster is the spider, Anansi. Folktales about Anansi were taken to the West Indies, where the character is often known as "Aunt Nancy." The oldest trickster tales come from China. There the hero is Monkey. He uses his tricks to defeat monsters. Because of this the gods allow him to keep on using his powers, but he is always getting into trouble.

EUROPEAN JOKERS

In Europe the trickster usually looks like a human, although he is able to turn himself into other shapes. He is Loki in Scandinavian myths. One story tells how Loki is asked to steal the necklace of a goddess.

He turns himself into a flea and bites her while she is asleep. She removes her necklace to look for the flea, and Loki runs off with it.

The most famous European trickster is Puck, from Shakespeare's famous comedy *A Midsummer Night's Dream*. In the play Puck finds a magic plant. When juice from the plant is dropped on the eyelids of people while they sleep, it makes them fall in love with the first person they see when they wake up. Oberon, king of the fairies, has an argument with his queen, Titania. To teach her a lesson, he drops magic juice on her eyes. However, as a joke, the trickster Puck has already given Bottom, the weaver, the head of a donkey. When Titania wakes she falls in love with—a donkey!

A trick goes wrong when Titania falls in love with a donkey in A Midsummer Night's Dream.

WHY WE NEED THEM

All these different world tricksters have something in common. People everywhere have often noted how events don't always turn out the way they should. For this reason humankind has had to come up with someone, or something, to blame for their troubles. Tricksters are really meant to represent the mysterious force or unknown "cosmic joker" that is said to make unexpected things happen. They help people to make some sense out of things that seem to have no scientific explanation.

CLOSER TO THE TRUTH

In recent years scientists have taken an interest in the unexpected. They have gone some way to explaining what the so-called cosmic joker might actually be. Mathematicians are working on something called "chaos theory." Some scientists are finding that different branches of math predict everything that happens in nature. The math is complex and difficult to explain, but it has to do with how what seem to be unrelated events actually affect, or have a great influence on, one another.

To give people an idea of chaos theory, scientists have come up with a simple example: "A butterfly flutters its wings in an African forest and, not long after, a hurricane strikes the Florida coast." This means that a tiny breeze created by the flapping wings of a small creature can move across the world, all the while gathering strength until it has become a hurricane.

A butterfly from central Africa. Could it have a part to play in the story of the cosmic joker?

Charles Fort, who came up with the idea of a cosmic joker, had described something like this. He wrote: "Not a bottle of catsup [ketchup] can fall from a . . . fire escape [in New York] . . . without it affecting the price of pajamas in Jersey City! . . ."

So, is the cosmic joker something that can never be explained? Perhaps some coincidences are just stranger than others. Or is there a scientific reason, such as the chaos theory, for the events described in this book? Humankind has yet to discover the whole truth.

Glossary

adopted Usually a word used to describe a child who has been reared and cared for by people other than his or her real parents. Also used to describe anything that somebody has decided to adopt, or take on, as part of their life, e.g. "He was not born here, but it is his adopted country."

adoption The act of adopting someone or something.

assassin A person who kills people for money, or for political reasons.

assassination The act of the assassin. "It was an assassination."

bizarre Something that is noticeably odd or very strange.

civilization Advanced human development in a particular time or place. "The Aztec civilization."

coincidence Two or more related events that happen by chance but which seem to have been planned.

coronation The ceremony to crown a king or queen.

cosmic Belonging or relating to space or the universe.

fiction Stories, or novels, about imaginary people and events. Also something that is untrue, or is a lie.

folklore The traditions, customs, beliefs, stories, dances, and art forms of people from different national groups.

hailstorm Frozen rain that falls to the ground as balls of ice and snow.

icicle A long hanging spike of ice formed by water that freezes as it runs down or drops off a surface.

kidnapped Abducted, or removed from a place, usually by force and against a person's will.

manuscript An author's typed or handwritten book or article.

mischievous Intentionally causing trouble but in a playful way.

Nazi A person belonging to Adolf Hitler's German Nazi Party, which controlled Germany from 1933-45.

psychic A person who claims to be able to see into the future, or who has other powers of the mind that cannot be explained by scientists.

teleportation Being able to move things over long distances without the use of any known force. Some people believe that teleportation is one of the basic forces of nature. However, scientists have not been able to find any proof that such a power actually exists.

terrorist A member of any political organization that uses violence— or the threat of violence—and kidnapping as a way of trying to force various world governments to give it what it wants.

Index

Further Reading

Bennet, Martin. West African Trickster Tales, "Myths and Legends" series. Oxford University Press, 1994

Brooks, B. The Sioux, "Native American People" series. Rourke, 1989

Hamilton, Virginia. A Ring of Tricks: Trickster Tales from America, the West Indies, and Africa. Scholastic, Inc., 1997

Weiss, Jacqueline S. Young Brer Rabbit and Other Trickster Tales of the Americas. Stemmer House, 1985

Wyatt. Amazing Investigations—Twins. Simon & Schuster Childrens, 1998